BOOKS BY ERIC PANKEY

Heartwood   1988
For the New Year   1984

HEARTWOOD

Poems by Eric Pankey

ATHENEUM *New York* 1988

Copyright © 1988 by Eric Pankey

Atheneum
Macmillan Publishing Company
866 Third Avenue, New York, N.Y. 10022
Collier Macmillan Canada, Inc.

Library of Congress Cataloging-in-Publication Data
Pankey, Eric, ———
  Heartwood : poems.
  I. Title.
PS3566.A575H43   1988   811'.54   88-6212
ISBN   0-689-70735-5 (paperback)
ISBN   0-689-11971-2 (hardcover)

Macmillan books are available at special discounts for bulk purchases for sales promotions, premiums, fund-raising, or educational use. For details, contact:
Special Sales Director
Macmillan Publishing Company
866 Third Avenue
New York, N.Y. 10022

10 9 8 7 6 5 4 3 2 1

Printed in the United States of America

ACKNOWLEDGMENTS

I am grateful to the editors of the following periodicals in which poems from this book, many in earlier versions, were first published:

Antioch Review: "Forfeiting Light"

Chester H. Jones Foundation's Award Anthology: "Apology"

The Christian Science Monitor: "Learning to Walk" (under the title "Trusting the Earth"); "Without Faith"

The Cincinnati Poetry Review: "By Dusk"

Denver Quarterly: "Ode to Forgetfulness"

Fine Madness: "Privilege"

The Gettysburg Review: "Debtor of Happiness"

Indiana Review: "Consolation"; "Overcoat"

The Iowa Review: "As We Forgive Those"; "Over His Sleeping and His Waking"; "Within a Circle of Rain, My Father"

The Kenyon Review: "Natural History"; "Permanence"

The Montana Review: "Reconciled"

The New Criterion: "If You Can"

The New Republic: "Into Happiness"

The Quarterly: "Family Matters"

Seattle Review: "From Danger"; "Snow on Ash Wednesday"

Seneca Review: "In Balance" (under the title "For the End of the World")

Shenandoah: "After It's Spent"; "Afterward"

Tendril: "Rhododendron"

Western Humanities Review: "Metaphor"

Sincere thanks are offered to the following people for advice on individual poems and earlier drafts of this book: Jennifer Atkinson, Marvin Bell, Mary Clark, Robert Crum, John Drury, Andrew Hudgins, Lisa Lewis, Barbara Molloy-Olund, and Jan Weissmiller.

Several of these poems were finished with the help of a generous grant from The Ingram Merrill Foundation.

"Crab Apple" is dedicated to Marvin Bell.

"The Road to Emmaus" takes as its source Luke 24: 1–44.

"The Debtor of Happiness" is dedicated to Robert Crum.

"Natural History" is dedicated to David Pankey.

"Apology" is after a poem, "Beyond Time," by Mieczyslaw Jastrun.

"Learning to Walk" is dedicated to Debby Petersen.

The painting that gave rise to "Metaphor" is *A Great Piece of Turf* by Albrecht Dürer.

"Hunger" takes its source from a story Anton Chekhov told his wife on his deathbed.

"Ode to Forgetfulness" is after a poem, "La Memoria," by Pablo Neruda.

"The Day" is dedicated to the memory of my father, James A. Pankey.

HEARTWOOD

for Jennifer

CONTENTS

HEARTWOOD

CRAB APPLE

The thin chipped branches of the crab apples,
    are as hard as anything
  that holds on beneath the iron cast
    of late autumn sky.

Whoever planted them as ornament
    must have loved the scattered nest,
  the broken-knuckled look of the thing,
    must have loved the fruit,

the unripe pithy white, the dusty red,
    some speckled with mold, some pecked
  but not eaten, the holes edged with black,
    black like charred paper.

If the trees are bent it is not from fruit.
    Each year they shrink a little.
  The ground beneath them goes soft with rot.
    The bark grays like shale.

You can only eat so much sour jam,
    and when you do you are left
  with the cramped, twisted look of the trees,
    a look so jagged,

you almost forget the season they flower.

THE ROAD TO EMMAUS

This is what they are offered. Their bodies, their eyes which fail
them. It is springtime. There is rain and the paths are rutted.

The gray mud along the road is a gravelly mortar.
There is an apple tree among the trees of the wood, light

in the rain-white smoke of blossoms. This is not suffering.
This is the story of what suffices, how the body

can be divided infinitely, how it can be held
like bread in the hands of a stranger, bread which is broken,

the dust of flour falling through the column of sunlight,
dust so finely lit it becomes nothing before their eyes.

WHITE HORSE

Those days as I drove over the rise
and my headlights hit the horse, I'd brake,
startled, believing the horse was loose.
It stood outside the short, tumbled fence.
By that time the sun would be up, but
the highway ahead of me still dark,
the hills falling away from the road
casting their shadows all the way down
the incline to the Cedar River.
All spring the horse had grazed the wide
ditch along Highway One, one leg tied
to a post in the ditch's center.
The white horse cut a perfect circle
in the rise and fall of weeds.
Today, driving that road again
after a summer away, I was already crossing
the bridge, sunlight breaking in flashes
behind the green paint and rust of support beams,
when I realized I had not seen the horse.
Ahead of me the slimmest of moons
persisted in the morning sky, white.
Perhaps the place where the horse had stood,
as round and hard as a threshing floor,
was now reclaimed by coreopsis, clover
and goldenrod. Or perhaps, the trampled earth
remained smooth and worn.
As I drove it was hard to know
which I would choose if it were my choice.

FORFEITING LIGHT

The hillside's red sumac,
A few thinning maples—
    So many trees lit up
Whole beneath evening's light.
    How long can the moon stay
Low like that, mildewed, cold?
    Its greenish burn on both
My hands surprises me.

    Glowing, phosphorescent
On a birch or white oak,
    In a thicket's shadow,
Lichen could easily
    Be mistaken—a ghost.
A spirit that returns
    Because I expect it
To. It is October.

    Below the ridge my car
Idles. The exhaust's warmth
    Burnishes the asphalt
A slick blue-black that fades
    Like his breath years ago
Damp against the mirror
    As I watched him shaving.
It was our time alone.

    I always thought someone
Climbing the oak across
    The mown field from our house
Could see us there—a boy's
    Face white with shaving cream,
A tired man splashing
    Hot water on his face,
Steam lifting from his hands.

6

Those hands touching his face.
The moon forfeiting light
    To the work-day morning.
My father not paying
    Attention as I played.
I believed that someone,
    Real or spirit, would watch
From that tree over me.

Now six months since he's gone,
In a season in love
    With death, I have stopped here
Beside these ragged woods.
    Li Ho was right—the trees
Do fill the four seasons
    With sadness. I'm home here
Where what is lost is loved.

DEBTOR OF HAPPINESS

Whatever empties the feeder
comes and goes without my knowing.
There is little satisfaction
in their names or the songs I've stopped
listening for. The birds that come
come in spite of me, are welcome
to rule the yard and its one tree,
to pick and scavenge the little
I've left them. I stood among them
once. The morning after Halloween
I broke open a frozen pumpkin
against the trunk of the maple
and chickadees and cardinals
and even a cedar waxwing
cleaned out the three jagged fragments
of their hard white seeds. Once I walked
along a river's marshy bank
pulling a canoe through the shallows
and all the sounds were water sounds:
the reeds swayed by wind, the wet call
of the killdeer, the heron's blue stealth.
Above the quick cut bank, sparrows
broke the air into flight like rain.

I believe the birds no longer
sing their one song of alliance.
If the hummingbird works its way
through the damp dust of evening,
if the black sweep of a crow's wing
or the jay's miserable crying
sends the other birds scattering
I am unaware. I feel the earth's
pull and cannot even look up
to see the nests in the winter limbs
or the hawk circle its hunger
above the rain-washed riverbeds.
Now in my dreams if I fly
flight is more like a falling.
I used to wake to their songs once.
I would listen and I would hear.
It was that simple. What I heard
wove a wreath in the air. I lived
beneath it like a happy man,
as if there were nothing, nothing but air.

NATURAL HISTORY

1.
Light settled in slowly like silt in the choked-off creekbed
until morning. Time passed like that.

After a long hunt for fossils in the scarped and silvery
clay of the bank

my brother couldn't decide
if the chipped finger-length stones we found

were the remains of marsh grass, or the spines of extinct fish
that lived so deep they were their own source of light.

But everything, he told me again and again, was turned
in time to calcium.

Pith or marrow. It didn't matter. He knew such truth.
He knew that sinkhole,

collared in black moss, where we sat listening to the deep
water's echo hollow in the distance,

might have been the bottom of the ocean.
He knew that the rise our house was built on

might have been a tidal island or a reef.
He knew that after the water receded, there was ice

and that wasn't the end of things. That's years ago,
he told me, before you can imagine.

2.

Summer nights, the grass not yet damp, we lay on our backs
and let the world, everything that held us down,

take us with it. The sky, each star locked in place, turning.
The heavens, we called it.

A machine we dreamed we invented,
so fragile it might break at our touch.

One night, after a week knotted with high winds, tornadoes,
we watched the clouds pile up,

the known dark above us collapse into blackness.
We believed God was up there, hidden. The rain broke

so suddenly we were soaked
before we could get to our feet.

Quick with lightning,
the rain and night flashed a moment of white.

That's what He looks like,
my brother said as we made our way to the porch.

Just like that.
Another stroke backed by thunder halved the changing dark.

We laughed, uneasy, our eyes blinded
as if we had seen Him. Just like that.

AFTERWARD

Three snow angels cast by the neighbor children
flaw the back yard and except for the footprints
it does look like something's fallen from the sky.
There never has been a more beautiful end
to the world.
               Each snow that fell in my childhood
falls again. Falls around me. But by lunchtime
the sun is out and the gray ice thins, breaks up,
exposes the shuddering black of the creek.
Always the day gave in to darkness. Always.
I take it all back. I meant it all. The words
that couldn't stop anything from happening.

OVERCOAT

The day my father came home, blood still wet
on his beige overcoat, the gash broken
open across his nose, raw and steaming
as he entered the house, it was Christmas Eve.

"I put the car in a ditch," was all he said
as he raised his hand to touch his wound, but didn't.
He was half-drunk and stood there like a child
needing help with the buttons on his coat.

I remember the water and soap, my hands
rubbed red as I worked the heavy fabric,
but the stain held fast, a splotch of brown
like mud outside where rain had worn away the snow.

Slumped on the couch, he talked himself through his sleep.
And as he slept, I drove from store to store
looking for the exact coat and when I bought it
I didn't have it wrapped. I even thought

of putting it on and stopping somewhere
to get dead drunk for the first time. I didn't.
He was half-drunk, which meant he'd wake easily
the next morning and remember enough

not to say a thing. He'd wake with crusted blood
along the ridge of his nose, with his coat
thrown over him as a cover, and know
I'd given it to him and that it was not a gift.

APOLOGY

I cannot help but be concerned with the age of those hemlocks
or the skiff held still on the frozen lake, an oar dipped beneath the
    ice,
or these weeds, the color of limestone, along the roadside,
or how long ago their seed crowns learned to quiver like that in the
    wind
or the cloud shadows to scout out the land's contour ahead of the
    storm.
For so long I kept saying *I'm sorry* to keep things safe,
to keep the dark from staying past dawn,
to keep the white weight of stars from pulling night down with it.
I believed the dream I woke screaming from—
all the world's water receded, leaving nothing but salt.
No one to take away the fever or thirst. A child's dream.
But I believed. I could taste salt on my lips, feel it in my eyes.
I could taste it in the words I couldn't help but say.
As today when I rub sage between my fingers only to find
a hard thread of wood, the words remain.

WITHIN A CIRCLE OF RAIN, MY FATHER

He waited for a light
that might save him. Gray,
the day spread from salmon
to gray. The dawn damp smoke,

the sky tipped and spilling
dark from the center, dark
blotting the far torn edge
until the whole day burned

whole. The static of rain
like scratches that shiver
white at a film's end, then
white fills up the blank screen,

that rain surrounding him
was the end of something.
And he could see the lace
which was the beginning

of light through the blue shreds
of his private circle
of rain. He could see light
sway the green-stemmed brush

and drift of bridal veil,
light catch on the ant-traced
buds of the peony.
That rain surrounding him

was the end of something.
As he moved to the light,
light that would have saved him,
rain filled in the spaces.

OLD BRICKYARD ROAD

If I remember right
the stacks of bricks, crumbling
into shards and red dust,
sunk deeper each year, tilted
into the clay and moss.
The line between the soft earth
and bricks was a gritty pulp,
a line stained with rusty mold.
If I remember right,
that was the first quarry pit—
seen from the sheer cut ledge,
half-full of rainwater, stale
and growing algae-green—
I convinced myself to dive
into, convinced that water
would be cooler than the day's
gathering heat and steam,
just to find what held me up
was as warm as the air
and yet dark. Hardly water.
I could taste lime, sulfur,
something green and going bad.
The muck, an almost-rot,
clear to the pit's dark bottom.
If I remember right,
a boy's body was found
by some railroad workers
dismantling the old track.
They found him on the shale
at the water's edge, his neck
broken, his body white
with dust. I can't remember
how many times I dove
that summer from the same ledge,
or what I felt standing
where the boy must have landed.

If I remember right,
that's when the barbed wire went up
around the old brickyard
and they started filling in
the quarry with garbage,
tree limbs, miles of railroad ties. . . .
If I remember right,
the fence kept me out.

PERMANENCE

Those days, I still say. Those days
as clear as light off frost

or the not quite magenta,
almost red of the peony

floating in the silver bowl.
Floating, then falling apart,

petals jostling silver
like lovely useless boats.

Dissolved like salt in water,
not lost? My own history

settles like fine sediment.
I can remember David,

my brother, upstairs adding
and subtracting. His world

shook by negative numbers,
that in truth there was something

less than zero. He proved it
on paper. Don't you believe

a thing they say, he warned. What
you take away is still there.

In the storm-wet charred remains
of an old tavern, the place

some folks said the mob burned down
and for good reason, I found

—because I was bored, nosey,
and early to work that day

for my job at All Nations
Capitol Flag and Banner

Company—in the rubble
a dead man. Foul play, I thought.

But it was just exposure.
He'd been there, I learned, for days.

Gritty light fell, filtered
through the pick-up sticks of beams.

On the dead man's hands and face
flecks of dried skin looked like ash.

The cops did not draw a line
of chalk around his body.

Get lost, kid. He's just a bum—
or was, the detective said.

Real as that rainfall. The past
swept up like woodsmoke, a glimpse

of mustard grass, violet dust.
Then the rain gives itself up.

The goodness of a splinter
that works its way in to stay.

I work all day long loading
fireworks into semis

and my hand hurts, but feels
good. The goodness that hurts.

Between stories, there's silence.
Within silence, permanence.

My father, the story goes,
didn't approve, but his friend,

a sergeant, was mad because
the sixteen-year-old whore,

my girlfriend, he called her,
was seen at *Kiyomizu*

arm and arm with a young man,
a Japanese. The sergeant

beat the kid as my father
watched. That night, this time alone,

the sergeant pulled the girl's bed
into the street and burned it.

He was crazy when he drank.
That's how the story ended—

with a laugh that was buffered
by a slow shake of the head,

my father's way of saying
it couldn't be helped. The bed

going up in flames, damp smoke
smudging the clear night. *Damage*

might be the title of all
the stories he told me. Each

a warning. A lesson learned,
told and retold. Unresolved.

These words like night caught in
the empty space of branches,

leaves full, but not reflected
in the creek's stillness. These words

like the few lights defining
the late dark of the back yard—

early fireflies, house lights
across the creek. The dark thick,

cloudless as water. The heavy
warm cloth of it over us

draped above the trees. Water
we are buried in and rise from.

When I was sixteen—*reborn*,
safe beyond reason—I wept,

empty of myself, giving
up, as they told me, this life

for the new life He promised.
Right there at the revival

held in the First Baptist Church
of Raytown, just like Jesus,

they told me, I wept. Cut out
the boo-hooing, my best friend's

father used to say, or I'll
give you good reason to cry.

And he would. I wished someone
would stop me, would give me back

my sin, what had slipped from me
like wind behind a curtain.

Just as I am, the choir
sang. Just as I am I come.

Take that one step, the preacher
said. This may be your last chance.

So I took my chance and wished
someone would stop me. I stepped

with care like a sleepwalker
who sees all that isn't there.

THE SAME CLOTH

Three rusted tines
wired to a broomstick
made the sticking end
of a frog-gigging pole.
Our father had shown
my brother and me how
to bring the prongs down
quick into the slick flesh
and hard cartilage
behind the bullfrog's eyes.
Then we would slip it
into a burlap bag
still alive enough
to kick in the darkness,
to beat like a heart
in the bag, until we
brought it home with us
and held it by its legs
and dashed its head hard
against a concrete step.
Then we'd slit the skin
with one pull of a knife.
With pliers we'd rip
the green mottled skin off
to reveal the legs'
pale taut flesh and blue veins.

The trick was to walk
through the puddles and marsh
silently, without
a splash or the suck-sound
the mud made when I
pulled my boots out. One time
when there was no moon
I stepped into a fall
of willow branches
and tangled up my spear.
I stumbled, sending
the chorus of bullfrogs
into the safety
of the scum-covered pond.
God damn it, I heard
my father say. That year
he and my brother
were the same height. I watched
their shapes through the trees
as they walked on. Light
from their flashlights cut
the dark quick like that
curse had. Then I saw
my father raise his hand
and hit my brother
as if he, and not I,
had ruined the hunt.

My brother kept walking,
his flashlight pointed
straight ahead, its beam all
dust where it ended.
That was not the day
when their anger began.
They're cut from the same
cloth, my mother used to say
as if that were cause
or reason. We had gigged
two frogs that evening
which wasn't enough
for a family meal.
At home, my brother left
to smoke with his friends.
My father washed his hands
and read the paper.
I sat on the back step
and watched the burlap
tumble and rock with life.
The first one took three
or four swings to knock out.
The second I slapped
harder against the step's edge.

PRIVILEGE

I confess that everything I've said has not told the truth
as clearly as the truth might be told. I confess I've failed

at lesser tasks. Just today, for instance, after the rain
gave way to a late summer sun and the yard went misty

with steam and heat, I thought I would see my father. I thought,
if this were a story he would be there, just like Jesus

walking beside the disciples on the road to Emmaus.
Before they recognize the risen Christ, they do not hide

their disbelief. They burden him with their suffering.
Today there was rain and afterward the rest of the day

to wade through. The year or so after my father died, when
my dreams were the kind I woke from feeling responsible

for suffering I had no right to claim, I saw my father.
I woke up and looked out my window and saw him standing

next to the jumble of tied branches and the raked remains
of the garden's tomato vines and peas. It must be cold out,

I thought, because he was standing there surrounded by rain,
and the window went from streaked to icy when I touched it.

I can honestly say it was my father standing there.
He was not a stranger. Whatever I might have said to him

went unsaid. The window filled with rain and the frost that formed
on the inside of the glass grew intricate, then opaque.

At Emmaus, it was not salvation for them to see
someone dead sit down at a table. I know my father

was not there to soothe or confront me, not there to offer
a second chance for me to say what I could never say,

a confession maybe, or something trivial and true.

ENDINGS

The end of the story he told,
although true, *the whole truth* to him,

felt false and full of the sleight of hand
of closure. His friends would agree

at the end of the evening
there would not be another night

like this one. One by one their guests
then said good night. It's not the end

of the world, she said to him
when later that night they argued.

And when she said that they both laughed
and it seemed the night was just

beginning. Are you happy? she said,
You know, really happy? He smiled.

Whatever he said would not
get it right. He let it end at that.

SNOW ON ASH WEDNESDAY

I was lazy last autumn;
I let the garden go wild,
let it fall in upon itself.
Now networks of stain hold on
like shadow to the white wall
of the shed where tomato
vines, fragile from winter,
crumble off the string lattice.
This morning near Saint Mary's
I watched slow heavy snowflakes
spiral down the chalk gray sky
and when the wind shot between
the church and parsonage
the column of snow shattered.
Flakes flew up like ash over smoke.
Ash is what I saw today
on the foreheads of children
who made snowballs on the steps.
Their mothers lingered and talked
beneath the high arched doorway.
The children waged their small war.
One boy, caught upside the head
by a throw, began to cry.
The charred cross above his eyes,
smudged, unrecognizable,
ran in dirty streaks along
his nose and onto his cheeks.
Above it all, pigeons chirred,
hidden in cornice shadow.
I expected the mothers
to be alarmed, or the birds
to lift from their white basin
of snow with a dull flutter.
But the boy just cried, his hands
soiled with his blessing.
I could do nothing for him.

Now the snow has turned to fine
cold rain. What remains unwashed
remains—all I am left with.
And that boy is no better
for his pain, for what he lost,
with his hard face in his hands,
tasting it all—salt, ash, ice—
what wears away at the world.

AS IT IS OF TENDERNESS

It is hard to get started
on a clear morning like this,
when what light there is
fills the room with an under-
water blue, when I wake and doze,
rock back into sleep and wake
with a start to my wife's cries.
Someone is stealing her child
in the danger sleep takes her through.
It's a dream she has often.
It is not her crying but I
who wakes her. *My love*, I say
with a voice as full of fear
as it is of tenderness,
My love. Then she turns to me,
tells me the damage sleep brought.
And the space our child fills
riding inside her body,
safe there, waiting to be born,
fills up the space between us.

TREES

for Jennifer

Sometimes you forget
and look to the trees.
The apple is there
darkened with its load.

You hear its limbs creak
in the slightest wind.
Or you are walking
through your father's woods

and the chestnut blurs
with blossoms of dust.
Those scrubby weed trees,
the names of which you

haven't cared to learn,
fill in whatever
light-stippled, needle-
mulched stretch of fire

path even the deer
haven't used in years.
The hemlock's shadow
remains a circle

beneath the noon sun
for an hour, remains
a circle of green
that is black as pitch.

You used to hide there
beneath the low sway
of the branches. Sometimes
the crazy birds thrashed

somewhere above you
and you woke unsure
of the season or
day. From the pine floor

you could smell autumn,
but there was also
rain, and the clean smell
of the woods after

an ice storm. Sometimes
you forget and look
to the trees for clues.
You might say their names:

Hazel, black walnut,
dogwood, juniper,
the tulip, the oak.
Their names are enough

to cast a shadow
in any season,
to cast away doubt.
The cut-back sumac

sends out a thicket
of thin green branches
from its hacked-up stump.
What you love about

the sumac is its
determination,
if you can call it
that, its will to grow

all knotted and bent,
odd, prehistoric
looking, the red tips
and the flat palm-like

leaves, all out of place
among the straighter
skyward trees. Think back
to any moment

in your life, to words
your father once said
in jest, words that hurt
you, to when you left

your closest friends
behind in your house
because they'd betrayed
you. Even though night

erased the trees' shapes,
you heard that water-
sound wind makes in trees.
You walked the graveyard

path and tried to name
each tree but could not.
You remembered ash
but the moon was gone.

Trees surrounded you
always, but sometimes
were little comfort.
Still the trees were there.

Think back and you'll see
a circle of green,
a ripe, woven wreck
of nightfall and leaves.

LEARNING TO WALK

The child next door is learning to walk
and steps carefully, awkwardly,
as if she didn't trust the earth,
as if it were not beneath her.
She steps as someone steps into water,
certain the clear surface gives way
to an unseen dark.
                              Sometimes she stands
and balances on her toes. Sometimes
she gives up and falls to the ground
but does not crawl. She kneels
with the side of her face
pressed to the ground,
with her hands pressed to the ground
as if she were listening
to the slow workings of a machinery,
as if she could steady the tumbling.
I am sure she is just resting.
This effort is tiring.
Still her attempt, her mastery,
deserves much exaggeration, much praise.

HOLE

When the tornado touched down,

the dark length of its tail
dragging the flat field

where we'd spent all morning
digging a hole

for no other purpose
than digging a hole—

the sheer sides of it
an exposure of sod,

clay and the intersection
of yellow roots through all the layers—

we watched the tornado's tip
at eye level

skid across the ground toward us,
and when the sky

and earth were as black
as one another,

we fell to our knees,
not in reverence,

but out of common sense
and were amazed

at the function
of the hole we'd dug.

ADOLESCENCE

I held on as it raced
along paths it made.
My back ached as I rode,
which meant I didn't know

how to ride, how to move
with the horse. I held tight
as it managed the ruts,
the root-tangled incline,

the crumbling ledge of sod
that traced along the creek.
I knew enough to duck
the pines' low-swung branches.

The girl at the stable
put me on the horse, said
to trust it, that the horse
knew what to do. All I

had to do was hold on.
So I held what I could.
The dancing reins, the taut
width of the horse's neck,

the saddle horn, the mane.
I rode and rode badly
through flashes of sunlight,
on paths and through thickets,

until I circled round
to the barn where she laughed
and the horse slowed and stopped.
I knew it was a joke

and the joke was on me.
I believed I could do
anything, like marry
that girl. As she laughed

I felt the horse breathing.
My legs lifted, lowered
more slowly as the horse
caught its breath. She squinted.

I didn't want to look
at her. She was eighteen.
So I watched the horse's
ears, how they eased and tensed

at some sound the wind brought,
how flawless they were, smooth.
I watched and said nothing.
I was still holding on.

METAPHOR

To capture the morning
    along the washed-out town road
above a slope too steep to grow crops
    he shoveled up this tangle
        of weeds and grasses—

each separate, clustered:
    feathery shoots of yarrow,
dandelion florets closed tight above
    their jagged damp leaves, cocksfoot,
        spare spikes of heath rush

and fleshy plantain.
    He carried it home before
the dew dried, before the green mass grown
    heavy with itself wilted.
        The sod in his hands

was wet and ragged
    with white tubers and nerve-like
roots. The dirt sifted through his hands
    fell in a trail behind him.
        Posed at eye-level

on a shelf above
    his table the square of earth
grew richer as he painted—
    creeping Charlie, meadow grass,
        clear for the first time

as the light, which was
    by now water and color,
dried still and permanent on paper.
    Springtime held in check, steadfast.
        A cool wash of green.

A *study*, he called
　　it later. An exercise
toward some greater painting. Perhaps
　　the wild growth among the rocks
　　of Calvary hill,

or beneath the head
　　of a waking guard surprised
by light from a tomb that bright morning
　　when spring arrived forever.
　　In this old story

about a painting,
　　in this long meditation
there is another, unknown story
　　about the young apprentice
　　who mumbled and bitched

as again he swept
　　the floor after his master
tracked in the red-clay soil, the straw
　　thrown down outside the doorstep.
　　When the boy stopped work

long enough to say
　　he had had enough, he quit,
the artist did not look up, did not
　　take his eyes off the green clump
　　losing its luster.

The boy cared nothing
　　for a mess of weeds, for years
of calculating the pure proportion
　　of head to hand to body,
　　the raw stink of oil.

40

Although his trained hands
    were skilled enough to copy
Christ's passion, a body in torture . . . ,
    he cared nothing for beauty.
      He wanted to be

a soldier, wanted
    to feel the taut right angle
of a bow-string as he released it
    shimmer into music.
      He wanted to go

to the Promised Land.
    So he gave up sweeping
and walked out into the clearing day.
    He walked the rutted roadway
      pocked with black puddles

south away from town.
    The old man could have his weeds,
he thought, stopping by the embankment
    from which the sod had been cut.
      It looked like what it

was—a scar of mud,
    not a grave's first shovelful
torn away. He did not believe in
    metaphor enough to see
      it as that, a grave.

FAMILY MATTERS

Drunk, she held her first granddaughter.
The woman swayed and laughed, lifted the child up

at arm's length above her head. When she fell
she fell in the slow motion in which all

accidents happen. Her son, who had just
entered the bedroom, caught his mother

around the waist, still he, the baby
and mother toppled together

onto the unmade safety of the bed.
In the end it was not the baby

he thought about—the baby would be fine—
but how he had to lift himself out between

his mother's legs like a man.

CONSOLATION

One story he always told
was a tale of loss—a crop
left in the field past harvest.
No help from the bank. The cold,

the clear frost claiming it all.
The man he'd hired to bring
in the corn refused and laughed,
"Doing free work is for fools."

That's when my father cracked
a beer mug against the man's
chin, breaking his jaw. —A lie
he told so often it was fact.

It felt good, he'd say, as good
as most things I've done. He'd wait
for someone to say something,
to say that we understood.

Now it's autumn. Or almost
autumn. Daylight lifting through
the early sky hard with chill.
The last long days burned and lost.

His loss stays in memory
like the dark sting and fragrance
of woodsmoke. Like his raised voice
when sleep would not cover me.

Already, the ease and ache
of morning. Another day,
he'd say as consolation.
Another day of hard work.

AFTER IT'S SPENT

I've watched the moon move through its wheel of smoke. I've watched
it turn into nothing, into the dark it filled.

The purple martin, the sycamore's mottled trunk
are background to the mist of the garden

and the clotted soil turned over to the rain.
The ground tilled but left unplanted, left to the weeds.

I've watched the parallel lines of furrows mark off
and measure the distance of the house's shadow

as it rides out and returns each day. The question
I woke with goes unanswered, but remains like snow

in the blue dark of gullies. Like evidence
of truth in a story composed entirely of lies.

STORYTELLING

I have tonight, as they say,
missed the boat. I've arrived late.
Already they have rowed out
to the center of the pond
as they do these nights to tell
the stories they tell, to drink.
Sometimes I join them. Sometimes
I wait too long—the last light
angles upward, yellow-white,
into my bedroom window,
the ceiling brighter than the day,
the rest of the room gone dark.
Instead of lighting the lamp
and working late as I should,
I walk out along the pond
and listen to my footsteps
move through dried weeds, through the rush
of new growth along the edge.
The creak and splash of oars.
A bottle dropped overboard.
Now that the sun is gone
and the distance between us
is an unmeasurable dark,
I can hear the men laughing.
Their calm, the stories they tell,
becomes a kind of music
in which it is the silence
I listen for, not the lives.
There is little I can hear
or even make out as words.
There are just voices, water's
hollow clap against marsh grass,
water nudging the wide boat,
and the quiet in between.
And there is relief in that.
Three of the men are miners.

The other, who no longer
joins them, sells farm tools
and sharpens scissors and knives.
Sometimes I see him at dawn,
his cough dulled to an echo
against the line of houses
as he walks beside his cart
and talks to his horse as if
it could reply with a laugh
or a nod, like his old friends
would when they rowed out at night.
He comes to see me sometimes,
still says he is feeling better.
Then he coughs. The blood-stained rag
he carries crushed in his hand
muffles the cough to a swathed rasp,
the damp sound of flesh tearing.
Sorry, he says, I'm almost
over this damn cold. Once spring
warms I'll be better. Really.
He'll be dead by late summer.
We both know it, but we lie.
Perhaps that is why he asked
me to take his place. The story
we tell each other ends well:
The two men part. They are not
friends, but know they could be friends.
The one walking away turns
and wants to wave, but does not.
The one standing at the door
lifts his hand, but instead
of waving scratches his head.
The narrator somehow leaves
the listener believing
in a certain happiness,
which is as much of sadness
as it is of contentment.

HUNGER

They watched a heifer eating
apples, and though pot-bellied,
in the waves of heat, it seemed
to float on the ripe sweet air
of the orchard. The woman
picked up a windfall, polished
it on the fine white linen
of her new dress, which she'd bought
just for this retreat. She liked
it in the country. She liked
to be able to pick up an apple
and make it shine. But when she
bit into it it was soft
and flavorless. It tasted
more like the mineral air
near the springs than an apple.
The man was hungry. The walk
had been long and tiring.
The road they'd taken followed
a field where men were mowing
oats. He felt dirty from the dust
and splintery chaff. He felt
like going back. I'm hungry
he told her and she reached out
and twisted an apple off
a low, gnarled branch. Eat this.
It will hold you until lunch.
His jaw ached from the hard green
sour of the fruit and yet
the man ate it core and all.
It just made him hungrier.
He talked of food as they walked
and his red cheeks grew redder.
He looked like a man who'd run
a great distance. Raw oysters,
veal stew with asparagus,

sautéed morels. The woman
could still taste the white tasteless
meat of the apple. I want
cherries, strawberries in cream,
orange- and lemon-flavored ice.
They talked like that, describing
wonderful entrées, desserts
all too rich to imagine.
I am hungry, the man said.
On their way they passed many
sights—the charred framework of a barn,
a horse kneeling in a field
as if it had fallen down
or been taken ill, a boy
in a thicket checking traps
but none filled them with beauty
and desire the way talk
of cod or a leg of lamb
made them feel their hunger, pure
undeniable hunger.
As they walked they passed one man,
but they did not say hello,
or even recognize him
as the chef from the resort.
The woman was creating
saffron rice as she talked
and the man was tasting it
as they took the flowered path
that led up to the resort.
The chef had argued again
with the owner and this time
he quit. There would be, of course,
no lunch or dinner today.

ODE TO FORGETFULNESS

You do not have to remember everything.

If you should believe that in the room where you
grew up the curtains were always drawn,
                      and if
you went back and found no curtains,
                      only blinds,
the frayed little noose hooked around a thumbtack,

if you should confuse *thirst* with *joy*,
                    if you should
call the taste of salt *bitter* when it is *sweet*
like the wind and the tired shoulders of water,

and if you spoke sweetly to your love and gave
her winter-blooming jasmine and took nothing,

what then? Should we pity you?
                      Remember
how easy it was to remember before
you were distracted by news of torture, frost
on the inside of the storm windows, the names
you might name a cat or dog if you had one?

One day you remember seeing your parents
making love when all you wanted was to ask
permission to cross the street.
                    One day the look
on their faces is one of exhaustion. Then
it is not a look at all, but a smell,
                    old
and damp like straw thrown down. They said to you, *Fine*.

On the road all fall the rolled hay bales steam,
                                        burn
slowly with their own heat. Like hunger, you think,
but know it's not right. You remember how barns
always seemed on the verge of collapsing.

To what can you compare your forgetfulness?
It is not a symptom of regret, a crime.

Both your brother and sister had collapsed lungs.
You're next, you tell yourself, but imagine
something worse and irremediable.
                                Not slow,
wheezing breaths, but a sudden panic because

you cannot remember the road you're on, or
the name of that mat of mown, dried grass that chokes
out even the weeds and grows thicker with their remains.

IN BALANCE

1.
A large torn branch, broken by wind
and caught in the netting of limbs,
dangles thirty feet up in the oak.
This calmer wind, after the snowstorm,
sways the black branch's loose end,
sends a pendulum of shadow riding
over the lawn, defining
the figure eight of its territory.
The woman across the street
yells to her boys to come in,
to wash for lunch. But they do not.
They have pushed the snow around all morning
into muddy balls and stacked
and shaped them into a snowman.
They are waiting for the heavy ice on the limbs
to melt, for the limbs to lift back up into place,
for the widow-maker to tip and fall.
Their mother calls again. This time with anger.
But something more dangerous than that
is held up in that tree, is held,
for the moment, in balance.

2.
I thought the end would come like this—
the snow turning to cold rain,

the dawn's little warmth packing the house in on all sides
with fog. Everything mist.

The trees are a haze of darkness and yet still trees.
What words are there except the words we know?

The hollow sound outside my window
is the wind fluting over the bamboo wind chimes.

Over the stalks. Over mounds of leaves
the rain has worn away until they glow in this light.

3.
The kitchen window, detailed with ice,
    keeps out the morning's darkness.
On the sill in full bloom and not yet
    failing, the forced paper-whites
are held and rise out of the shallow
    earthen pots we placed the bulbs
in, already now, a season ago.

We hid them in the unused garage,
    covered the windows and bulbs
with black plastic and waited. We knew
    that we could trick them to life.
They were something for us to believe
    in—the bulb's shattered flesh,
the entire life held whole in there.

OVER HIS SLEEPING AND HIS WAKING

Here, he thinks was a kingdom. The leaf he crushes
crumbles into dust, woody threads and hard edges.

And the wind that scatters it is the same old wind
that blew before the ruining, that blew over

everything. Over his sleeping and his waking.
What was once a kingdom. Once he believed it all

his own. Each day and night a landmark on a map.
What he had forgotten was like a washed-out road.

Here—beside the splitting trunk of a Chinese elm,
its line of hard bark and wound sap, its weight pulling

itself in two, the skirt of leaves and damp plowed earth
of the earth and grubworm—here, he thinks, I begin.

RECONCILED

1.

Ahead, the fire path ends—all deadfall and loam, stones the wall has given up, deer shit and hoof marks.

A few bleached leaves still cling—almost white, a white stained ivory, yet bright against the late winter's mottle—to the pin oak's spindly branches.

Parallel rows of birch I cannot call cathedral are ruined, some still standing, some torn and toppled showing the hollow and rot the paper bark kept in.

The thicket of raspberry and tumble of leafless sticker bushes seem hardly a barrier at all.

I hold my four-month-old child against me, against the wind, and we do not go on.

2.

In the Arizona desert with my father, once, we came upon what he said was an abandoned mission—four crumbling walls and a courtyard of hard pan and shards of tile.

The wind, funneled through the arched doorway spun up a twist of dust that disappeared against the evening sky already opening to stars and chill.

I lost count of the falling stars I saw and have forgotten most of whatever history he tried to teach me.

This is what I remember: We shared the quiet.

I was the age when everything was emblem—the empty bell tower, the ground's branching cracks which ran outward from wherever I stood, the glow as my father took a drag on his cigarette, the shadow of the crater's edge.

3.
Lead-blue, the sky, as heavy as that, yet cloudless, chalked in from edge to edge, appeared neither ominous nor hopeful in its emptiness, its clarity.

It was Thanksgiving Day.

Our daughter had been born the night before—first her head, then the length of her gray-blue body followed.

I walked beneath that noontime sky and the more I searched the hungrier I got—everywhere the smell of a feast being prepared—but no restaurants were open.

At home, I ate alone and slowly with the appetite and embarrassment of one who starts eating before the host has said grace.

FROM DANGER

Sometimes the day stalls, but does not falter
caught here in the after-dawn.
                              I'm awake
and cannot recall the words I've said,
the shout that woke me, words that called me back
from danger. I remember low storm clouds,
the dream-sky poised above me like a hand

and then it all comes down.
                              Sweet dreams,
my mother would say each night, standing there
long enough to make the words magic. And true.
When I'd look she'd be gone.
                              The doorframe empty.
The light from the hallway cut into the dark
like a wing. I'd watch the slow swirl and dance
of dust held in the light and I'd be asleep.

Sometimes now I wake before the end
of the fall I am falling in my sleep,
the boards beneath my box spring rattled from my weight
and the sky that's fallen with me.

I sit up and watch the morning start, cold and bright,
waiting for enough warmth to give it lift.

I am a child in the dream.
                              And someone,
on the other side of the avalanche of blue
that has knocked me off my feet, wishes me well.

INTO HAPPINESS

Just last week I was bent with sickness.
It's the flu, I told myself, meaning

it would go away as quickly as it came.
Meaning I'd live. And I did.

Just last week the winter was relentless.
Now, in the gutter right next to my feet,

rivulets of thaw scrawl in the gray silt.
I don't understand how it comes to this—

shaded drifts gutted by wind, snow retreating,
blackening into mud, the bright light dazzling us

into happiness—how this is all a healing.
Just last week my body burned like a useless fire.

Someone says, How are you? I say, Fine.
And my body hardly recalls its pain.

It's over, one of us says, meaning winter.
When just last week there was no trickling of water

to leave its scars or scribblings
on the exposed earth, to touch us with its damage.

WITHOUT FAITH

Last evening I walked down toward the Missouri
through the cool shadow of the bluebell wood,
through last light guttering in the leaves and black pine.

Ahead where trees end raggedly,
give way to sweet woodruff and azaleas,
I heard the shudder and break of pheasant.

I stepped fast to see them, their wings thrashing
air and underbrush, turning it into flight
—a quick dart and arc into nightfall.

But they were gone. The low rhododendron
where they'd hidden shivered still.
I felt the wind rise over

the warm worked air of their escape, the shimmer
of gathered night dew on the waxy leaves.
I stood there long enough to believe.

THE DAY

Everything was as he remembered.
The day ahead of him green and tough
as nettles. The day would last all day.

It was as if he had been frugal,
as if he had been responsible
for saving up the hours to come.

He believed that when the day arrived
the world would be so calm
that even those who had a warning or sign

would merely watch the evening come on
as if it were the evening before
a long journey. Still, he longed for

the patience of the day. The shadow
of the maple crossing the window,
the room going light to dark to light.

The room that looked out on the day
he believed was his own. Everything
was as he remembered but still

he couldn't tell what had changed and what
had not. He watched the early sky fill
the surface of the flooded meadow.

He watched the swoop of swallows, the hard
branches of the fruit trees roughed by wind.
He watched. And watched in patience. He watched

and betrayed nothing and no one.
Although he was not, he felt at home.
The day ahead of him was enough.

BY DUSK

By dusk the greenwood burned,
no flame, but a smudge of smoke
the wind pulled up taut as a wire.

Hardly a fire at all. A stutter and spit
at the center as I poked at it
with a stick. But fire enough to sit around.

Beside us, in that darkness,
the Missouri was still.
We watched the smoke in its integrity

rise up into the globe of darkness
above the broken edge of the limestone bluffs.
We watched it linger and rise

into a quiet, like the soil-sweet breath
a knife releases as you cut a melon.
What I believed then, believed to be happiness,

is no less true. And if the testament
were written, my one true sin
would be that I believed imperfectly.

And in that book it would be a lesser sin,
weighing less than the gray soot of smoke
from a fire we could not coax into flame.

RHODODENDRON

Winter. Chickadees make their way
from the snow-tipped shrub to the feeder.

I admire them—their resilience,
their nervous flitter a measure

of the morning's minutes. Familiar
fright, full of greed and clear impatience.

They take the given as if stolen.
One after another, but never

more than one risking flight at a time.
The hedge quivers. The feeder sways.

I remember that quick scene as mine.
A green life full of too many hearts.

AS WE FORGIVE THOSE

You're excused, my father would say.
                              My father
was last to get up from the dinner table.
When I heard the word I heard its rhyme *accused*.
All my life I was a child. I waited
for someone to say my name. I stood in lines.
I learned to forgive from those who forgave me.
I can't remember now if I was supposed
to forgive those who trespassed, or my debtors.
Trespass was what I did for apples, for fun.
I stole green tomatoes and dropped them from trees.
I crouched behind low junipers, waited,
my bare knees on the brown dried prickers, bagworms
hanging as thick as the hard blue berries, waited
for a glimpse of someone naked, a crime,
something only I would see and know.
                              That year
in school I learned the word *omniscient*.
I learned other words as well, but what I loved
were the words that no one would ever use.
We always owed someone or someone owed us
and that's why we didn't talk about money.
I don't think we ever used the word *debtor*.
Give us this day we would say in that prayer
as if the day were not already ours.
When I'd come home and find my parents yelling,
they would tell me not to worry; it didn't
concern me.
              That's what I thought forgiveness was.
Being excused from something you knew nothing
about. Sometimes I'd wake and hear them talking,
kindly, intimately, with the care one takes
when a baby is asleep in the same room.
Those were nights I'd pray, nights I'd talk aloud
so I wouldn't have to listen to my heart
go about its business.

I prayed for knowledge,
although those nights I couldn't have called it that.
I knew there'd be something for which I'd be blamed.
I knew someday I'd stumble unknowingly,
if I hadn't already. I knew enough
to pray for something possible. I said *Give us*
this day and when the night passed the day was there.
I walked out beneath the maple that ruled
our house half the day in sunlight, half in shade.
Its shadow swept every inch of what we owned.
When it covered me I knew I was forgiven.

IF YOU CAN

for Clare

In your life you will bruise your heel.
You will be walking some day and step
down hard on a sharp rock.

Whether you cry or curse or just feel
pain shiver up your leg, you will take
your next step with more care.

You waited a long time to be born.
We waited with you, waited for you
in this world full of rocks.

Once I believed I was saved, beyond
the trouble my family, my friends
and my own stupid choice

brought me. But saved by whom or for what
I don't know. But somehow I was.
If you can, please, believe.

It does not make the rocks any less
hard. It is not like ice which fills cracks
and shatters rocks into dust.

But it makes you feel a tenderness,
like blood cushioning the hurt, a bruise.
It shows us where the pain is.

64

ERIC PANKEY was educated at the University of Missouri and the University of Iowa. His first book, *For the New Year*, received the Academy of American Poets' Walt Whitman Award in 1984. Since then, he has received grants from the Ingram Merrill Foundation and the National Endowment for the Arts. He teaches and coordinates the Writing Program at Washington University in St. Louis, Missouri, where he lives with his wife, Jennifer Atkinson, and their daughter, Clare.

ACQ-46666

2/14/9(_)

PS
3566
A575
H43
1988